A Ladybird Bible Book

Elijah and Elisha

Text by Jenny Robertson
Illustrations by Alan Parry

Scripture Union/Ladybird

‘No one in Israel cares about God any more,’ thought Elijah sadly. ‘Everyone’s been praying to foreign gods ever since King Ahab built a temple to his wife’s special god Baal. As if golden statues could help them! Only God can do that. I’m going to tell King Ahab that he must change his ways.’

Barefoot and dressed in rough skins, Elijah strode off over the hills. Grey clouds hid the sun. The rainy season was about to begin.

Elijah walked all the way to King Ahab's fine palace with its richly carved furniture and its floors set with ivory. He spoke to the king in a voice like thunder.

'I've heard how you've tried to kill everyone who won't worship your wife's god Baal,' he said. 'But I still serve God and I've come to tell you that God, not Baal, is in control. And as proof of that there won't be any more rain, not even a dew-drop, until God says so!'

He turned and walked away, his bare feet padding softly over the beautiful floor, and the king and the queen stared after him in fury. They decided to kill him but Elijah went quickly into hiding.

God kept Elijah safely hidden in a valley near the River Jordan. A brook ran through the valley so Elijah had plenty of water. But he needed food too and nothing grew on the bare hills around him.

'I'll send some ravens with food for you,' said God. And every morning and evening ravens flew into the valley carrying bread and meat for Elijah in their beaks. He always had enough to eat and stayed safely in the valley until the brook began to stop chattering over its stony bed. Soon there was only a trickle of water. Then it dried up completely.

'God hasn't let it rain,' Elijah thought. 'Now perhaps the king will believe in God and stop worshipping Baal. But I shall die here without water.'

'Leave the valley now,' said God. 'Go to the coast. You'll find a new friend there who will look after you.'

It was a long journey. The ground was so hard and dry that all the crops were withering. Elijah felt hungry and thirsty when at last he arrived at a small village near the sea.

A poor woman came along gathering sticks.

'Please, could you bring me a drink of water?' Elijah asked. As the woman turned away to fetch some water he called after her, 'Could you bring me a piece of bread, too? I'm so hungry.'

The woman stopped. She was almost as poorly dressed as Elijah, and he could tell that it was a long time since she had eaten a proper meal.

'I've not a scrap of food in the house,' she said. 'And that's the truth. All I've got is a handful of flour in the bottom of my barrel and a drop of oil. I'm gathering sticks to light a fire so that I can bake a pancake for my little son and myself. That's all we've got to eat and then we'll have to starve.'

'Don't be afraid,' Elijah said. 'Go and make your pancake but make me a small scone first, please. God will look after you and your son until it starts to rain and there'll always be flour in your barrel and oil in your jar.'

The woman hurried home. Soon she rushed back to Elijah. 'Here's your scone, sir! And it's true! My barrel's full of flour. Come and stay in our house now.'

So Elijah stayed in the woman's house and there was always enough to eat even though it didn't rain at all.

Three years later God said to Elijah, 'Go and tell King Ahab that I'm going to let it rain.'

So Elijah told Ahab to get together the priests who served Baal and all the people on a mountain called Mount Carmel.

'We're going to see who the real God is,' he said.

Once everyone had arrived Elijah told them to build an altar to Baal. They built an altar, piled firewood high on top of it and heaved a bull on top to burn as an offering to their god.

'Wait a minute. Don't light the fire yet,' called Elijah. 'Pray to Baal. If he's really a god he'll send fire to burn up the bull.'

All day the priests and people prayed to Baal but not a spark fell out of the sky to kindle their fire. Elijah watched and laughed at them. Finally he told them to stop.

'I'll build my altar now,' he said. 'But I want you to pour water over my firewood until it's too wet to burn. Then we'll see who is more powerful, God or Baal.'

Then Elijah prayed to God, 'Lord, prove now that you really are the God of Israel. Answer my prayer so that everyone will believe in you.'

Immediately the sodden wood on Elijah's altar began to hiss. A flame spurted high. The wood crackled as the fire blazed. Everyone bowed to the ground chanting, 'The Lord really is God.'

Then they killed the priests who had led them to worship Baal and Elijah turned to the king, 'Go and eat now, King Ahab. I can hear the rush and roar of a great rainstorm.'

But the sky was still blue and there wasn't a cloud to be seen. King Ahab sat down and ate a meal while the people scattered to their homes. But Elijah climbed to the top of Mount Carmel, taking a servant with him. He knelt and prayed, his face bowed down on the earth.

'Now have a look out towards the sea,' he told his servant.

The servant scanned the horizon. 'There's not a cloud in the sky,' he called.

'Look again,' said Elijah. 'Look seven times.' The seventh time the servant yelled. 'There's a small cloud no bigger than my hand blowing up from the sea.'

'Then run and tell King Ahab to drive off home before he gets soaked,' called Elijah.

The sky grew dark and the wind howled over the mountain tops, driving storm-clouds across the sky. A few drops of rain spattered the earth. The king jumped into his chariot. His driver urged the horses on but now God gave Elijah such strength that he went racing down the mountain faster than the chariot and ran on through the downpour ahead of the king.

When the queen heard that Elijah had killed all the priests who served Baal she was furious and sent him a message. 'By this time tomorrow you'll be a dead man!'

Elijah fled for his life. He ran into the desert until he could go no further. Finally he hid under a bush.

‘I can’t go on any more,’ he groaned. ‘Let me die, Lord.’ He was so tired he fell asleep. Suddenly he felt someone touch him and started up in alarm. An angel stood in front of him. ‘Get up and have something to eat, Elijah,’ said the angel.

Elijah sniffed. There was a good smell in the air. A loaf was baking on hot stones close by, and a jug of water stood beside it. Elijah had some bread to eat and went back to sleep. The angel woke him again. ‘Eat and drink, Elijah. You’ve got a long journey ahead and you need food.’

Elijah finished the bread and travelled on through the desert. It took him forty more days to reach the holy mountain where long ago God had given Moses and the people their Law.

It was getting dark and Elijah took shelter in a cave. There God spoke to him. 'What are you doing here, Elijah?' asked God.

'I'm distressed because I'm your only faithful follower,' said Elijah. 'And now they are trying to kill me.'

'Go and stand outside,' God replied.

Then God sent a wind tearing over the mountain. Rocks rattled down the slopes and the storm seemed to be blowing the mountain apart. Elijah watched for God but God wasn't in the storm.

Then the wind dropped and the ground began to shudder. An earthquake made the mountain rumble and shake under Elijah's feet, but God wasn't in the earthquake.

The shaking stopped. Flames leapt among the rocks and fire crackled through the long dry grass. Elijah shaded his face from the heat and the glare but he didn't see God in the fire.

Then everything became very still and God spoke in the quietness. Elijah covered his face with his cloak and went out of the cave as God had told him to.

'Don't think you're the only one in Israel to follow me,' came God's voice. 'I have seven thousand other true followers who don't worship Baal at all. I can make even kings carry out my plans. But I know how lonely you feel, Elijah, and I am giving you a friend, a man called Elisha. Go and find him. He'll help you now and carry on your work some day when you have gone.'

Elijah set off in search of Elisha and found him with eleven friends, ploughing, each man guiding two oxen yoked to a wooden plough. As Elisha came by Elijah reached out and tossed his cloak across Elisha's shoulders.

Elisha understood. He left his plough and ran up to Elijah. 'I'll be your helper but let me

go and say good-bye to my family,' he said.

'Of course,' Elijah agreed.

Elisha hurried back to his plough. He killed his oxen and chopped up their yoke and the plough for firewood. He roasted the oxen and shared a good-bye meal with his family and friends. Then he walked away with Elijah.

Elijah and Elisha worked together teaching people about God until the time when Elijah knew that God was going to take him away. He didn't say anything but Elisha knew that something unusual was going to happen.

The two friends walked to the banks of the River Jordan. Then Elijah hit the water hard with his cloak and a path appeared for them to walk across.

'Ask me one last thing,' Elijah said.

'Leave me a double share of your power to help me carry on your work,' Elisha replied.

'That's hard,' said Elijah. 'But it will be yours if you see God carry me away.'

They walked on. Suddenly a splendid fiery chariot pulled by flaming horses flashed between them and whirled Elijah away.

But Elisha saw him disappear and he cried, 'My father, I've seen our country's strong chariot and the horsemen who guard us, but you have gone and I won't see you again!'

He ripped his clothes to shreds in grief. Then he noticed Elijah's cloak on the ground. Elisha picked it up and went back to the Jordan. 'Help me, God, as you helped Elijah,' he prayed and hit the river with the cloak. The water swished back as it had done before and a startled crowd on the other bank watched Elisha walk across the river. They all came and bowed before him.

Elisha travelled about the country with his servant Gehazi. There was a rich woman who invited him for a meal whenever he came to her village.

'Elisha's one of God's servants,' she told her husband. 'Let's make him a spare room on the roof so that he can rest here whenever he comes by.'

Elisha was very grateful and wanted to do something for her in return.

'She would like a baby,' Gehazi said. 'She and her husband have no children.'

So Elisha told her that God would give them a baby and to her delight she had a son.

A few years later the little boy went out to watch the harvesters at work in the fields. The sun was very hot and he suddenly clutched his head. 'Father, help me, I've got such a headache,' he cried.

A servant took him home to his mother and he died in her arms.

She carried him to the spare room and laid him on Elisha's bed. Then she saddled a donkey and rode away to find Elisha, who came back at once. He went into the spare room and shut the door. First he prayed and then he stretched himself on top of the child, pressing his face against the boy's face until the cold body grew warm. Suddenly the boy sneezed seven times and opened his eyes.

His mother was overjoyed. She bowed to the ground, thanking Elisha and then carried her child back downstairs to tell everyone the good news.

Elisha helped people whenever he could and because he trusted God he could often do very wonderful things.

Once while Elisha was teaching a group of very poor people about God, Gehazi his servant started to cook their dinner. Food was very scarce and they hunted for herbs and berries to make their stew go further. One man found a wild vine laden with fruit. 'I don't know what this is, but there is so much fruit it will help fill us up,' he thought. He picked as much fruit as he could carry back with him, chopped it up and put it all in the pot.

But the fruit was poisonous.

'We'll die if we eat this,' the men cried when they tasted the stew. 'It's been poisoned. What can we do?' they asked Elisha. 'There's nothing else to eat.'

'Don't worry,' Elisha said. He picked up some flour and added it to the cooking pot. 'It's quite safe now,' he assured them, so they all enjoyed the rest of their meal.

Sometime afterwards a famous army commander from another country, Syria, came to Elisha for help.

The commander was called Naaman. He won a battle against Israel and among his prisoners was a little girl. He took her home to his wife to be her servant.

One day Naaman's wife told the girl some sad news. 'Naaman is ill. He's got leprosy. No one can make him better and he'll have to go away and live all by himself in case anyone else catches it. Oh, dear, whatever shall we do?'

'I wish he'd go back to Israel,' said the servant girl at once. 'Elisha could make him better, I'm sure.'

So Naaman asked the king of Syria if he could go off to Israel. 'Of course,' the king agreed. 'I'll send a letter to the king of Israel. Go straight to him. I'll tell him he must cure you.'

Full of hope Naaman set out, taking silver and gold and fine clothing as presents for the person who would make him better.

But the king of Israel tore his clothes in dismay when he heard what Naaman wanted. 'This must be a trick! The king of Syria is trying to start a fight! Of course I can't cure anyone.'

But Elisha sent the king a message. 'Send Naaman to me. I'll show him that God is still at work in Israel.'

So Naaman rode off to Elisha's house.

Elisha didn't even come out to meet him. He sent Gehazi instead.

'My master says you must go and wash seven times in the River Jordan and you'll be cured,' said Gehazi.

Naaman was furious. 'I haven't come all this way to be told to go and have a wash!' he exclaimed. 'Besides we've got two fine rivers at home. Why can't I wash there instead of in this muddy river?' And he rode away in a temper.

But his servants begged him, 'Sir, please do what Elisha wants. After all, if he'd asked you to do something difficult you would have tried it at once.'

Naaman calmed down. He waded into the River Jordan and dipped under seven times and washed himself. When he came out every trace of leprosy had gone and his skin was smooth and soft again.

Naaman rode back to thank Elisha but Elisha refused any of his expensive presents.

'Well then, just let me tell you, sir, that I believe in your God now and I'll never pray to any other god again,' declared Naaman.

Elisha smiled. 'Go home in peace,' he said.

So Naaman went home to his wife and her slave girl and Elisha went on with his work for God.

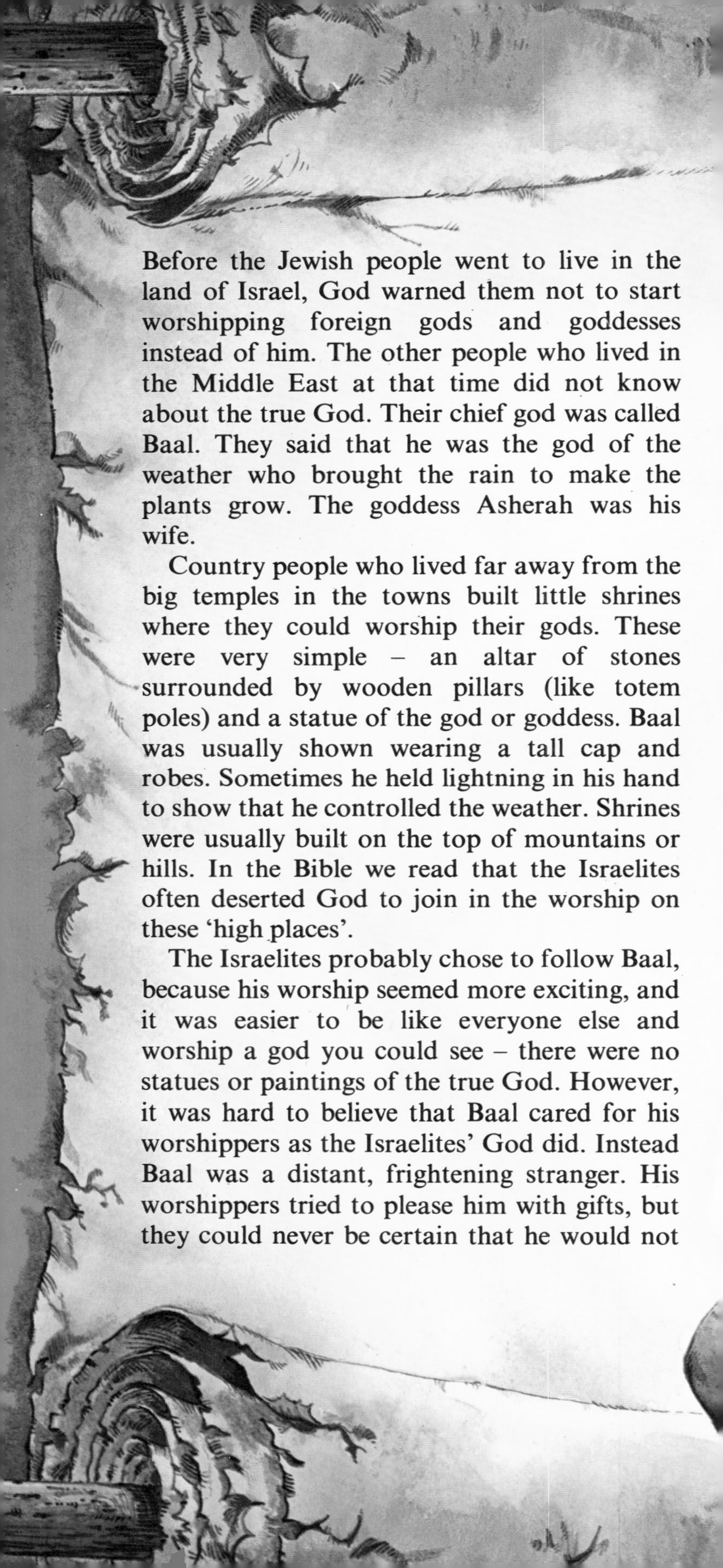

Before the Jewish people went to live in the land of Israel, God warned them not to start worshipping foreign gods and goddesses instead of him. The other people who lived in the Middle East at that time did not know about the true God. Their chief god was called Baal. They said that he was the god of the weather who brought the rain to make the plants grow. The goddess Asherah was his wife.

Country people who lived far away from the big temples in the towns built little shrines where they could worship their gods. These were very simple – an altar of stones surrounded by wooden pillars (like totem poles) and a statue of the god or goddess. Baal was usually shown wearing a tall cap and robes. Sometimes he held lightning in his hand to show that he controlled the weather. Shrines were usually built on the top of mountains or hills. In the Bible we read that the Israelites often deserted God to join in the worship on these 'high places'.

The Israelites probably chose to follow Baal, because his worship seemed more exciting, and it was easier to be like everyone else and worship a god you could see – there were no statues or paintings of the true God. However, it was hard to believe that Baal cared for his worshippers as the Israelites' God did. Instead Baal was a distant, frightening stranger. His worshippers tried to please him with gifts, but they could never be certain that he would not